MW01231585

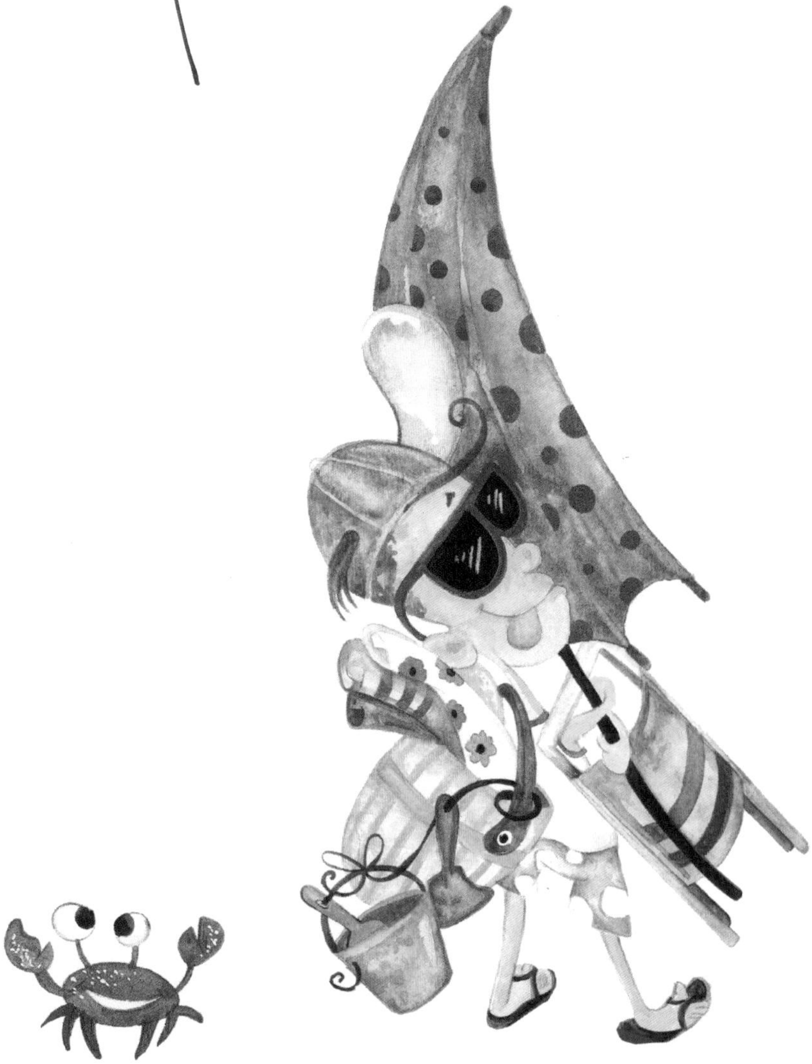

When
Fred The Snake
and Friends
Go to the
Beach

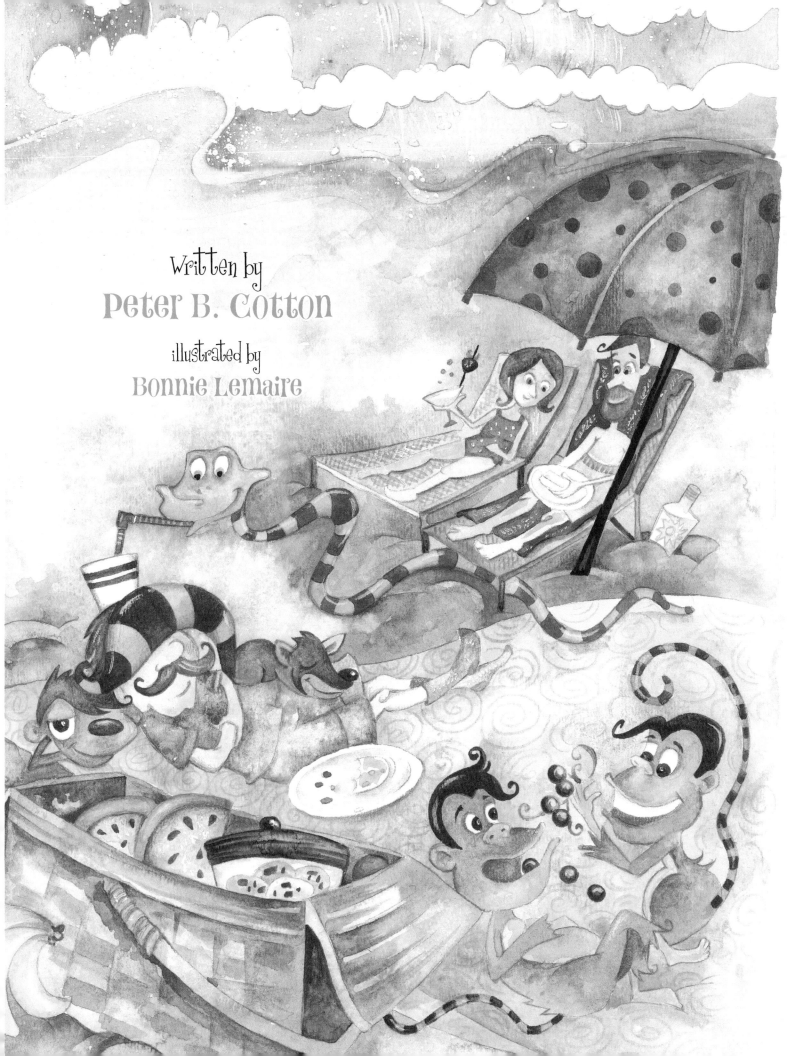

Written by
## Peter B. Cotton

illustrated by
## Bonnie Lemaire

www.petercottontales.com

Book design by CDesign Graphics

This Book Belongs To:

_____

DEWEES ISLAND

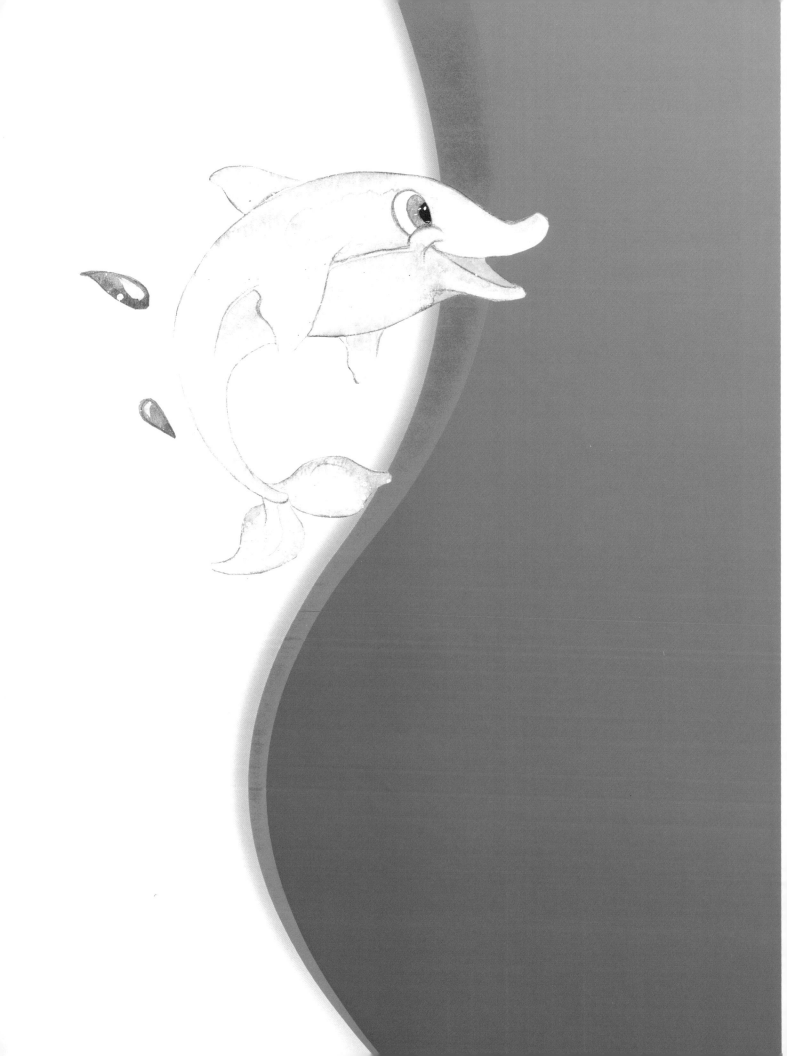

This book is dedicated to my wonderful family, and all friends of Fred.

Remember Fred the friendly snake,
who was squished once, by mistake?
But he was never really sick,
and got mended double quick.

He learned
his lessons
well in school,
and made
playground
things so cool.

Then Fred invited Jungle Jim,
who brought lots of friends with him.
Soon they all found, there's nothing finer,
than to be in Carolina.
Then spent happy days and nights,
exploring all the Charleston sights.

I wonder what will happen next.

Then Jack the boy received a text.

Maybe it's my Daddy, please,

he's been teaching overseas.

Yes it is, hip hip hooray,
my Daddy's coming home today!
Jack asked the tall giraffe,
to keep a lookout down the path.

Very soon our
Dad appeared.

Wow, he's grown
a bushy beard!

He hugged Mama, young Jack too,
and met our whole new household zoo.
Where's your sister? Perdy's away,
it's her school excursion day.

Daddy said, "let's have
some fun, enjoy a day
out in the sun.
The forecast is for lovely
weather. Get our beachy
stuff together".

You'll need swimsuits,
towels and mats, and don't
forget your floppy hats.
Lather on the sunscreen
please, on your face
and neck and knees.
We will go down to the sea
at Sullivans or IOP.
But Jack said, oh Daddy
please. Let's go over
to Dewees.

DEWEES ISLANDER

14

OK. We'll take the ferry,
now, be quick, say hello
to captain Rick.
He gives us all an easy ride,
and soon we reach
the island side.

There's our golf cart, 44, we will take
it to the shore. Jim, please help us for
a start, by hitching up the big wheel cart.
We'll need buckets and some spades,
and umbrellas to give us shades. Pack some
chairs and games to play, bocce, frisbies and
croquet. And, you very helpful loaders,
don't forget the snacks and sodas.

Drive down that road and soon
we'll reach, the track that takes
us to the beach.

There's a good place for our camp,
at the bottom of the ramp.
Put the chairs down side by side,
not too close to the rising tide.

Daddy said, all come with me,
let's go swimming in the sea.
Bernadette and Fred take care,
here's a boat that you can share.

All the others one by one,
came to join them in the fun.
The monkeys want to ride the bikes,
and the parrots should fly kites.

Jack was trying hard to ride,
two dolphins swimming side by side.

And Jungle Jim was very brave,
surfing an enormous wave.

Everyone, now lend a hand,
to make a castle out of sand.
Build the walls, and turrets tall,
carefully, don't let them fall.
Decorate with shells,
and you, should dig a
moat around it too.

It will look really fine,
filled with bucketloads of brine.
Plant a flag on top now, please,
and let it flutter in the breeze.

25

Mama said that you'll be a winner,
if you're bringing home our dinner.
So, Dad took out his fishing gear,
announcing, never-fear
we will answer Mama's wish,
by reeling in a great big fish.

Very soon we heard a shout,
Daddy's caught a great big trout.

Jim hurried off to get,
a suitable big landing net.
Measured it with a ruler,
and packed it in an icy cooler.

Cooler

Look, is that a turtle track,
going up and curving back?
If there's a nest, maybe,
it could be hatching, let's go see.

We watch the baby turtles scurry,

to the water in a hurry.

Avoiding all the seagulls, which,

see them as a tasty dish.

Thinking dishes makes our Jack,
ready for his teatime snack.
There are sandwiches with jam,
and slices of the sweetest ham.

Cheese balls, goldfish, and, wow,
lookie, a really yummy looking cookie,
that Mama made, and bottles
of pink lemonade.

A beautiful fun day to share,

but suddenly a horrid scare.

Fred, did you forget, to keep an eye on Bernadette?

The tide has turned, and with its motion,

took her way out in the ocean.

We are worried. Oh, brave Jack,

please find a way to bring her back.

Parrots, go calm her if you can,

while we make a rescue plan.

Jack borrowed Daddy's surfing kite,

and, holding on with all his might.

Skimmed across the sea so fast,

and reached dear Bernadette at last.

Maneuvering the mighty sail, he swooped,

and grabbed her by the tail.

Together back to shore they flew,

to happy Fred and all the crew.

Now it's cool,
the sun is low,
and time for
all of us to go.

Pick up the
trash and
all our stuff,
it looks as
though we
brought enough.

36

Call the ferry with your phone,
we'll be needing a ride home.

From the deck we all can see,
playing dolphins, two or three.

Putting on a pretty show
in the lovely sunset glow.
Thanks to Mama, Jim and Dad,
for all the special fun we had.
Home together now, we're on our way,
it's been a very lovely day.

**D**r. **Peter Cotton** was born in Herefordshire, England, where his father was a country physician. He was educated at Cambridge University and at St. Thomas Hospital Medical School (London), and graduated as a doctor in 1963. He eventually became a Gastroenterologist, and ran a leading department at The Middlesex University Hospital in London, before moving to USA in 1986 to become Professor of Medicine at Duke University in North Carolina. In 1994, he moved again to set up the Digestive Disease Center at the Medical University of South Carolina in Charleston. He recently retired from clinical work but continues part-time in research and teaching. He has written many medical textbooks, almost 1,000 scientific papers, and recently published his memoirs entitled *The Tunnel at the End of the Light: My Endoscopic Journey in Six Decades.* (www.peterbcotton.com)

Peter Cotton first wrote about *Fred the Snake* for his then young children almost 40 years ago, but publication began only after he found a perfect illustrator partner, Bonnie Lemaire. (www.bonniella.com)

*When Fred the Snake Got Squished and Mended* was awarded the "Best Rhythmic Book" prize by a New York company "Story Time Jam—This Book Rocks" in 2013. The first three books together won the "2014 Moonbeam Children's Book Awards bronze medal for "best picture book series", and in May 2015 the *Midwest Book Review* kindly commented, "Move over for Fred-Fred, Lewis Carroll."